ANARCHY AND REVOLUTION

■ ■ ■

A PROPHECY

Prince Handley

University of Excellence Press

Copyright © 2016 by Prince Handley
All Rights Reserved.

UNIVERSITY OF EXCELLENCE PRESS
LOS ANGELES · LONDON · TEL AVIV

Printed in the U.S.A.

ISBN-13: 978-0692613238
ISBN-10: 0692613234

First Edition

The only "Anarchy" book you need!

INTRODUCTION

Right now, the world is at a precipice. Basically it has to discern **"the illusion of safety" versus "the reality of control."**

Control is a multi-faceted serpent:

- From the guardian to government.

- From the streets to sanctuary.

- From the counselor to courts.

- From the priest to politician.

Gang violence and government abuse are but opposite ends of the spectrum with as many types of players as dynamics in between. **There will arise soon across the landscape of Planet Earth a schism of anarchy and government control.**

This book will present you with the answer. It is NOT for the passive or weak; but only for those who desire to be "power players" in the last days of Planet Earth.

SPECIAL MESSAGE

In this book is a dream prophecy from God that will impart spiritual DNA into your whole being. And then ... YOU will be able to bring about true and organic revolutionary change to Planet Earth.

O:O ☞

Prince Handley

ANARCHY AND REVOLUTION

■ ■ ■

A PROPHECY

INTRODUCTION

A few years ago many of us saw the video of a young teenager—an honor student—who was murdered by other teenagers in Chicago. His name was Derrion Albert, and I am dedicating this book to Derrion and his family.

FIRST, let me say to you that I have the answer to gang violence and anarchy—and everything that juxtaposes itself with opposition to abusive government. Let me give you a few examples:

Gene Browning was a Black Muslim who hated whites. He was an all state football tackle. On Saturdays Gene would go to the park with his Doberman Pinscher dog and wait until a white person would come by with their dog. Then Gene would turn his Doberman loose on them.

Hungry for the truth, Gene turned his life over to the REAL Jesus (not the Muslim Jesus) and became a dynamic Christian leader working with university students. Later he started ministry in government circles and prisons (is there any difference in the two anymore) as a Bible teacher and as a commodities broker in Washington, D.C. Gene and his wife, Shirley, gave me a beautiful automobile as a gift of love (even though I'm white!). That's REAL redistributive wealth!

Tom Skinner grew up in Harlem, and was influenced by the Black Nationalists, a Black supremacy group. He became leader of the Harlem Lords gang in New York City and led the gang in more than fifteen large-scale gang fights—and they never lost—even though there were only 130 in the gang. Tom was preparing strategy one night for what was to be the largest gang fight ever to take place in New York City. (Five gangs were

6

uniting together to fight a bunch of gangs from the other side of the city. If he succeeded in leading the gang bangers to victory in this fight, he would emerge as the leader of this alliance of Harlem gangs—the most powerful teenage gang leader in the city.)

Tom heard a preacher—*while he was planning the largest gang fight in NYC*—unexpectedly while listening to a DJ on the radio. As a result he decided to put Jesus' claims to a test. He was confronted with the revolutionary truth and **gave his life to the real revolutionary: Jesus, the Messiah of Israel.**

He quit the Harlem Lords and later started evangelistic meetings in his own turf, Harlem, at such places as the Apollo Theater. The Lord groomed Tom so that he had opportunities to speak to—and influence—countless individuals, groups, and organizations, ranging from members of Congress to the New York Yankees to officials at IBM Corporation. He also served as chaplain for the Washington Redskins. Some of Tom's publications are:

Black and Free
Words of Revolution

The Crips Gang in Los Angeles used to have several of their members who came to my Bible studies on Friday nights. They were invited to the study by a teacher. Many were touched and changed by the POWER of the Holy Spirit.

Also, I used to pastor an all Black church in the Compton-Watts area of Los Angeles. I was the only White person there. We had a music director who taught in the public school system and he was instrumental *(a play on words)* in bringing many students to church.

Clayton Joyner, an African-American, was my best friend. We used to preach together to the Black Panthers and the Black Muslims and the gangs in downtown Los Angeles. Clayton was black and I was white (still am). Blacks and Whites and Hispanics and Asians finally got used to Clayton and I hugging each other and praising God in the open air. When Clayton would buy a new suit or sport coat he would buy a suit or sport coat for me (I usually didn't have any money).

Finally, years later I was able to give him an automobile. That's REAL redistributive wealth!

Bob Selby was a friend of mine who was a gun runner and weapons stock-piler for the Weather Underground (close associates to Obama before the Whitehouse). Bob was reading literature while in jail that showed him that **there was a real Hell and that God loved us and sent His own Son, Messiah Yeshua, as the sacrifice for our sins**.

Bob prayed and gave his life to Christ in that jail. He later went to the Sheriff and took him to where this cache of munitions and guns were stored. I later had the privilege to speak in "standing room only" crowds in Carlsbad, California (USA) for Bob and telling young people about the REAL revolutionary: Jesus, the Messiah of Israel.

These examples I have just given prove that **there IS an answer to gang warfare and inner city violence … and anarchy**.

SECOND, let me say the government will NOT do anything about political corruption that breeds abuse and anarchy except fund programs and allow photo-ops like the one I saw in Chicago with **Attorney General Eric Holder** who wouldn't even go visit ground zero. He was safely in the swank Four Seasons Hotel off Michigan Avenue meeting with "community leaders."

If Obama had enough interest in his own home town as he did in flying to Copenhagen, he would be a man and go talk to the gang bangers in Chicago ... at least reach out to them. He would do something about it. (After all, it's a shorter flight to Chicago than Copenhagen ... or does commercialism outweigh needy children? What happened to PURE socialism?) Never expect socialists to be realists unless the money flows to them.

I noticed Obama's pastor, **Rev. Jeremiah Wright**, wasn't active in reaching out to the gang bangers ... nor was Obama's associate for helping the oppressed in his neighborhood, **William Ayers** (Weather Underground / FBI watchlist).

However, it is obvious the President was only interested in programs that can advance his socialist agenda. Like other socialists such as Karl Marx and Friedrich Engels, it appears that Obama was NOT really interested in the people—even needy children in his hometown—except as a tool of the collective for promoting his own socialist programs.

Nor was **Rahm Emmanuel** willing to "hit the turf" until the turf demanded his resignation. Ask the "bangers" what they think of Chicago politics and Obama's cronies.

Before you judge me for my statements, let me say that **I love the President. I pray for him and his wife, Michelle, and their daughters, Malia and Sasha, every day**. (How often do you pray for them?) If you love someone you will speak the TRUTH.

Years ago, during a demonstration, I obtained permission by the Sergeant of Arms of the California (USA) State Capitol to put up a large sign with a **Star of David** and the words in Hebrew and English:

MESSIAH JESUS
DIED FOR US
WAS BURIED
IS ALIVE

Below the sign on the portico were 7,000 college and high school students attending a "spiritual revolution" rally where one of the speakers was Al Hopson, a Black evangelist who had worked with several Black Panthers. I later had the privilege to minister with him at an international conference in San Diego (USA).

It's interesting to see who the REAL spiritual leaders are—*mostly behind the scenes*—in the Black community. For example, in the summer of 2015 in Hartford, Connecticut (USA) the **so called "Reverend" Al Sharpton** asked for money from unemployed blacks to donate $100 each to his ministry because of the recent gang shootings—**more than a dozen in a month in 2015**—where NO white people were involved.

Thankfully, one black pastor, Pastor Marcus Mosiah Jarvis, got up and vocally opposed Sharpton. The unemployment rate there had ranged from 16.8% down to 11%. Pastor Jarvis, shouted out to Sharpton, *"How dare you ask the people of Hartford to give you their money! You're nothing but a pimp!"*

THE ANSWER — A PROPHECY

While in prayer during the writing of this message, I had a vision—**it was actually a prophecy**. The vision was of a dry, extremely parched, land. It was so parched that there were deep cracks throughout the land where the dry ground had separated due to lack of moisture. The deep cracks were consistently spaced every foot (30 centimeters) or so apart, with smaller cracks between them. It was truly a "dry barren land." However, **in the middle of the land there was a fresh bright stalk of corn** with ears ready to open and leaves luxuriantly bright from perfect nourishment.

Then, **from the stalk of corn** there began to come forth not only its own fruit (other ears of corn) but ALSO moisture which watered the dry parched ground ... and then, to my amazement, other stalks of corn began to rise up from the ground and to grow and flourish.

Then God spoke to me:

"This is a picture of the future of many people [who will read this book]. Many are productive now ... but nothing compared to what will be happening through them in the future.

13

On the other hand, many have given up; they once had a vision that I gave them for their ministry. Some of them have seen others fulfilling what they once prayed and fasted about doing, seeking my face for the fulfillment of the same.

But the enemy of mankind and of all righteousness has discouraged them. He has spent years planning attacks against them, even using those who at one time were their friends, companions, or fellow ministers. Some of them have fallen due to sin, disobedience, misunderstanding, and attacks due to jealousy of enemies; and, some of the enemies have been My people.

But I am about to rearrange the lives of the faithful ones: the ones who have persevered. They are going to be like the fresh bright stalks of corn with ears ready to open and leaves luxuriantly bright from perfect nourishment.

I, the LORD, have seen their discouragement and disappointment. **I have seen the attacks of the enemy, even the attacks of My people against them**. And just as Joseph's brothers meant it for evil, I

14

MEANT IT FOR GOOD THAT I MIGHT SAVE MANY PEOPLE spiritually, mentally, and physically.

I am about to deliver many people—masses of people, hundreds of millions of people—from among the nations, tribes, and families of the earth. *Tell My people there is hope—to seek my face again—and to START NOW. I will use them GREATLY and in ways they have not expected."*

That is the vision and the message the Lord gave me. Now ... if that applies to you, where do you go from here?

1. START NOW

It doesn't matter if your ministry is one of the five-fold gifts to the church as apostle, prophet, evangelist, pastor, or teacher ... or whether you have the ministry of helps ... or whether you are involved in a labor of love that is hidden from the eyes of many.

You are to START NOW believing God for the anointing upon the work you are doing to bring torrential rains of the Spirit upon mankind. And PRAY that it is multiplied around the world. Get

15

SERIOUS about yourself, your ministry, and your influence!

"Behold, the former things are coming to pass, and NEW things do I declare: before they spring forth I will tell you of them." [Isaiah 42:9]

The Hebrew word "**chadash**" for "**new**" here means exactly that: "**new, fresh, a new thing.**" **The God of Israel doesn't deal in stale commodities; He is the Creator**. He is going to create NEW works through you ... and He will get ALL the glory. You and everyone around you will know it's not you.

The Holy Spirit is God's agent on Planet Earth to supply the resurrection power of Messiah Yesua. START NOW asking God what you can do to be a "nesting place" for the Holy Dove. If nothing comes to mind right away, then start with humility!

2. FIGHT

God is telling you to start now, and that means **He is going to help you and that nobody can successfully withstand you**.

"What shall we then say to these things? If God be for us, who can be against us?" [Romans 8:31]

The Greek word "**kata**" here for "**against**" denotes "**opposition, distribution, or intensity.**" Many times the devil will distribute evil agents to oppose you, **with the goal of destroying you and thereby nullifying the work of God through you**. Sometimes these agents will attack you from different sources and avenues simultaneously. Since **the NEW work which God will be doing through you is GREATER than anything you have been involved with in the past**, the opposition is [*super*] naturally going to be greater.

This verse in Romans 8:31 is literally telling you in the original language in which it was written that God regards YOU as the very chiefest—very highly—and for YOUR SAKE He is FOR YOU!

If you're experiencing weariness then cast it away in Jesus' name. It is no more than an attack of Satan: **a lie of Satan to get you to believe you can't go on**, that you can't take on any NEW work(s). If you are plagued with gossip as a result of past sins or disobedience then turn to your Father in Heaven and remind yourself of His love and forgiveness. Just remind God, yourself—and the devil—of who you really are.

Say this, *"I am the righteousness of God in Christ."* Then remind the devil of his future (burning in Hell forever). If you're experiencing doors shut to you by men and committees of men, rejoice. Those **shut doors are just direction for you into the GREAT OPEN DOORS** of ministry for God in these last days!

But since you KNOW that God has commanded you to START NOW and that He is FOR YOU, then all you have to do is be willing to FIGHT the good fight of faith. **Stop global whimping!** Stand up and fight. And, **after you have done all ... STAND**.

"Wherefore take unto you the whole armor of God that you may be able to withstand in the evil day, and having done all, to stand." [Ephesians 6:13]

The Greek word "**histaymee**" here for "**stand**" means "**to continue, covenant, establish, hold up.**"

3. BELIEVE

The only one that can cause you to lose is YOU!

Jesus said unto him, *"If you can BELIEVE, all things are possible to him that believes."* [Mark 9:23]

Put some MIRACLES in your account. **Use your faith to put supplies and people (everything and everyone) you need "in trust"** ... that is, in **YOUR heavenly bank account** ahead of time. That's what the word "**believe**" in Mark 9:23 means [**Greek "pisteuo"**]. Have FAITH ... establish some credit ahead of time ... by believing and receiving what you need ahead of time. Be specific!

"Therefore I say unto you, Whatever things you desire, **when you pray, believe that you receive them**, *and you will have them."* [Mark 11:24]

The word "**lambano**" here for "**receive**" means "**to take, to get hold of, attain, obtain**." The SECRET is **WHEN YOU PRAY!** That's the TIME to RECEIVE! When you're in your prayer closet that's the TIME to receive those BIG things from God ... some may come into play years later ... **but you receive in faith NOW**—WHEN you pray—and you SHALL have it!

Later in the day, the devil will try to challenge your faith and tell you: *"Those things you prayed for this morning are TOO BIG ... God isn't going to do that for YOU!"* That's when you want to say to the devil, *"Thank you, Mr. Liar, for reminding me that I RECEIVED those things in my prayer time this morning; now I KNOW I have them ... Jesus—The Truth—promised me."*

The only one who can cause you to win is YOU! God is already FOR YOU; that is a given fact! You KNOW this—now YOU are the one who must do your part: **START NOW ... SEEK HIS FACE ... FIGHT ... BELIEVE ... ACT!**

4. DREAM BIG

Dream BIG ... it may be your last chance!

"Call unto me, and I will answer you, and show you great and mighty things, which you know not." [Jeremiah 33:3]

My transliteration of Jeremiah 33:3 is as follows:

"Call God out by His name, cry out ["qara"] *to Him, pronounce to Him your cause. He will pay attention to you with His eye and respond to you* ["hanah"] *by announcing His answer. He will manifest to you boldly* ["nagad"] *exceedingly great things* ["gadol-gadol"] *that are strong and inaccessible* ["batsar"] *to you except by His miracles."*

"Now unto Him that is able to do exceeding abundantly above all that we ask or think, according to the power that works in us ..." [Ephesians 3:20]

How BIG can you ASK?

How BIG can you THINK?

Start challenging God. Quit insulting your Father. **Give your Heavenly Father the opportunity to show you Who He is!**

Litigate. Go to the Heavenly Court. Plead with God. Tell Him you are wanting to be involved with His program to bless the nations: to reach the world for Messiah Yeshua.

Tell Him you won't take anything LESS than every nation, tribe, tongue and dialect for your Lord!

"Put me in remembrance: let us plead together. You make a declaration, so that you may be justified." [Isaiah 43:26]

5. LIVE HOLY

Set yourself apart so that you can be used for "special" works for the Lord.

"If a man therefore purge himself from these [dishonorable practices], he shall be a vessel unto honor, sanctified, and meet for the master's use, and prepared unto every good work." [2 Timothy 2:21] **"Sanctified"** [Greek: **"hagiazo"**] means **"purified or consecrated**."

Resist the devil. Realize the enemy's tactics. Remind yourself, *"The enemy is a liar and a loser!"* **Give glory to God by living holy**.

Through holy living you accomplish the following:

- You please God;

- You establish a testimony;

- You enable yourself to be used for "special" works.

EXHORTATION

For those of you who are "starting again," let me encourage you. **You will be stronger this time**. You will have the "eye of the tiger." **The enemy will never take you captive again—and he will never take you alive!** You've already been close to death at the hands of the enemy. **You will never let it happen again. You will be one of God's key generals**. You will serve Him out of love, appreciation, and thanksgiving.

If God used Moses (who was a murderer and repented) and if God used King David (who was both an adulterer and murderer who repented), then God can use you! On the last day of his life Samson killed more of the enemy Philistines than he did in the previous times of battle. **Let God avenge you for the times the enemy has wounded you!**

"For the Lord God will help me, therefore shall I not be confounded. Therefore have I set my face like a flint, and I know that I shall not be ashamed. He is near that justifies me; who will contend with me? Let us stand together: who is my adversary? Let him come near to me. Behold, the Lord God will help me; who is he that shall condemn me? Lo, they all shall wax old as a garment; the moth shall eat them up." [Isaiah 50:7-9]

"And even to your old age I am He; and even to grayish-white hair will I carry you. I have made and I will bear; even I will carry, and I will deliver you." [Isaiah 46:4]

"Behold, all they that were incensed against you shall be ashamed and confounded; they shall be as nothing. And they that strive with you shall perish." [Isaiah 41:11]

I trust this message will stir you to **let God use YOU** in bringing about TRUE revolutionary change in society and in the world.

Here's a book that will help you to be
a **real revolutionary** in the End Times:

PROPHECY, TRANSITION & MIRACLES

BONUS

To help you, and to help you teach others, we have prepared FREE **Rabbinical Studies** at this site:

uofe.org/RABBINICAL_STUDIES.html

The above are commentaries from **ancient** Jewish Rabbis that identify the Mashiach of Israel.

Also, to help you, and to help you teach others, you will find Bible Studies in English, Spanish and French.

▎ English FREE Bible Studies

uofe.org/english_bible_studies.html

▎ Spanish FREE Bible Studies

uofe.org/spanish_bible_studies.html

▎ French FREE Bible Studies

uofe.org/french_bible_studies.html

OTHER BOOKS BY PRINCE HANDLEY

www.realmiracles.org/books.html

- Map of the End Times
- How to Do Great Works
- Flow Chart of Revelation
- Action Keys for Success
- Health and Healing Complete Guide to Wholeness
- Prophetic Calendar for Israel & Nations: Thru 2023
- Healing Deliverance
- How to Receive God's Power with Gifts of the Spirit
- Healing for Mental and Physical Abuse
- Victory Over Opposition and Resistance
- Healing of Emotional Wounds
- How to Be Healed and Live in Divine Health
- Healing from Fear, Shame and Anger
- How to Receive Healing and Bring Healing to Others
- New Global Strategy: Enabling Missions
- The Art of Christian Warfare
- Success Cycles and Secrets
- New Testament Bible Studies (A Study Manual)
- Babylon the Bitch – Enemy of Israel
- Resurrection Multiplication – Miracle Production
- Faith and Quantum Physics – Your Future
- Conflict Healing – Relational Health
- Decision Making 101 – Know for Sure
- Total Person Toolbox
- Prophecy, Transition & Miracles
- Enhanced Humans – Mystery Matrix
- Israel and Middle East – Past Present Future
- Anarchy and Revolution – A Prophecy
- The "Spiritual Growth" Series (several volumes)

AVAILABLE AT AMAZON AND OTHER BOOK STORES

UNIVERSITY OF EXCELLENCE PRESS
LOS ANGELES · LONDON · TEL AVIV

www.ingramcontent.com/pod-product-compliance
Lightning Source LLC
Chambersburg PA
CBHW060606030426
42337CB00019B/3628